PRODUCT LIABILITY
A Multibillion-Dollar Dilemma

Stephen M. Settle
Sharon Spigelmyer

AMA Management Briefing

AMA MEMBERSHIP PUBLICATIONS DIVISION
AMERICAN MANAGEMENT ASSOCIATIONS

Library of Congress Cataloging in Publication Data

Settle, Stephen M., 1950-
  Product liability.

  (AMA management briefing)
    1. Product liability—United States.   I. Spigelmyer, Sharon,
  1954-   . II. Title. III. Series.
  KF1296.S4   1984   346.7303'82   84-18512
  ISBN 0-8144-2308-6   347.306382

© 1984 AMA Membership Publications Division

American Management Associations, New York.
All rights reserved. Printed in the United States of America.

This Management Briefing has been distributed to all members enrolled in the Insurance/Employee Benefits Division of the American Management Associations. Copies may be purchased at the following single-copy rates: AMA members, $7.50. Nonmembers, $10.00. Students,$3.75 (upon presentation of a college/university identification card at an AMA bookstore). Faculty members may purchase 25 or more for classroom use at the student discount rate (order on college letterhead).

First Printing

About the Authors

Stephen M. Settle is the director of loss prevention and control with the National Association of Manufacturers, where he coordinates the association's efforts on compensation law, product liability, safety, and health. Mr. Settle has been very active on NAM's behalf with the Product Liability Alliance, a coalition of associations and corporations seeking reform of the product liability system.

He was graduated in 1981 from The George Mason University School of Law, where he served as business editor of the Law Review. He is a member of the Virginia State Bar Association.

Sharon Spigelmyer is the senior associate director of human resources and equal opportunity for the National Association of Manufacturers. She has also directed media efforts on behalf of product liability for NAM. Prior to joining NAM, she was a lawyer with Melvin Belli's office in San Diego, where her caseload emphasized product liability, personal injury, and medical malpractice.

She was graduated from the University of San Diego Law School in 1982, and is a member of the California Bar and the American Bar Association.

Contents

Preface

Product liability prevention is an exercise in judgment. Informed judgment will lead to good prevention programs which, in turn, will reduce liability exposure. Specifically, careful management decision making concerning product safety and liability control procedures can:

- Yield some reduction in product liability litigation costs and burdens by reducing preventable accidents;
- Place a company in a better position to defend itself against any product liability claims;
- Help the company guard its reputation and product marketability against the adverse public opinion that accompanies litigation;
- Improve the economic stability of the company through improved risk assessments;
- Improve the company's ability to comply with existing and future government regulations affecting its products; and
- Enable the company to negotiate more favorable product liability insurance rates or opt for alternative insurance schemes.

This briefing presents some of the causes of increased product-related litigation, the trends toward increased liabilities for manufacturers and product sellers, and the solutions being proposed to remedy deficiencies in the current legal system. It offers some suggestions on how to translate legal duties and trends into affirmative preventative safeguards.

1

The Spiraling Product Liability Crisis

Billions of products pour into the American marketplace each year. The vast majority have been tested, retested, and tested again for quality and safety. Yet each year more than 20 million injuries occur from use of those products. And of those millions of injuries, the National Commission on Product Safety estimates 30,000 persons die and another 110,000 injuries result in permanent disability. Still more people incur serious injuries or are killed in workplace-related accidents.

These staggering figures continue to increase each year. Not, however, because of manufacturers' and sellers' lack of attention to the matter of safety. The fact is that quality control has never received more attention than in the 1980s. First, businesses' sales and reputation are at stake. Second, foreign competition has increased pressure to compete for quality and price superiority. Third, federal and state laws mandate minimum standards of quality control. Fourth, insurance premiums depend on minimum exposure to risk. And finally, lawsuits involving product "reliability" are soaring in numbers, amounts of awards, and litigation costs.

Today, litigation is becoming a more and more prevalent part of doing business. The number of product liability suits filed in federal district courts alone has increased 500 percent in the past eight years.

Product Liability: A Multibillion-Dollar Dilemma—9

That's nearly three-and-a-half times faster than the average annual increase in civil suits filed in federal courts. It is estimated that similar, and probably even larger, percentage increases have occurred at the state level. In 1960, there were fewer than 50,000 product liability suits filed in the U.S. Just how many product liability suits are filed now is unknown, but figures range to one million a year.

Not only is the number of product liability suits skyrocketing, so is the size of the verdicts. In 1978, a California jury awarded a record $127 million to a man seriously injured in a car accident in a case involving one of America's largest automobile manufacturing companies. Nineteen-eighty-four witnessed the settlement of the "Agent Orange" case by seven chemical companies for $182 million. Some claim that the allocation of money to veterans exposed to the toxic substance dioxin saved thousands of lives. Multimillion-dollar verdicts are becoming commonplace.

And the verdicts only reflect a portion of legal costs. A recent Rand Corporation study revealed that nearly $2 goes to legal services for every $1 that actually goes to the claimant. A small brake manufacturer, testifying before the Senate Commerce Committee in 1984, said it was legal costs, not awards to injured parties, that accounted for his high product liability insurance. He said that his company's insurers paid out $850,000 for product liability claims in 1983. Of that amount, about $700,000 went to lawyers and for transaction costs. In other testimony, sporting goods industry representatives said they had been driven out of business because of the increased cost of defending ludicrous, as well as legitimate, cases.

The increased costs of defending lawsuits results in increased insurance premiums. These costs are generally passed on to the consumer through increased prices. The result has been that U.S. companies are having a tougher time competing internationally. A recent study revealed that insurance premiums for product manufacturers and sellers in Europe and Japan are about 20 to 100 percent less than they are the in the United States. While product liability premiums are hardly the sole reason for America's declining role as the world's premiere exporter, they are a factor.

The spiraling number of lawsuits, which result in higher insurance costs, is in large part due to a major development in the law—a development which has eased the burden of proof necessary to find a manufacturer or product seller responsible for an injury. We have moved from a legal system that held manufacturers liable if they acted "unreasonably" to a system which holds them "strictly liable," with little or no regard to the care used to manufacture a product.

Not only have the laws been weighted toward strict liability, but all 50 states have different standards for evaluating product liability. This disparity in state laws prevails despite the fact that only about 30 percent of the goods manufactured in any one state are consumed there. The result is not good for consumers, either. Under the law in one state, a person will be able to recover $2 million. In another, given the same facts against the same manufacturer, the same person will not recover anything.

Many of these varied laws, manufacturers find, do not encourage companies to enhance safety or to improve products once defects are discovered. The reason? Because evidence of improvements may be used in some states as proof that the product was never safe in the first place. And if a manufacturer is to be held strictly liable, no matter what safeguards are taken, there is little motivation to enhance safety features.

Manufacturers and others in the product distribution system believe that the development of new products that improve the quality of life and enhance life expectancy will be hampered if the laws are not revised. Society, through its laws, will have to balance all interests to decide overall goals for product safety and product development in the next decades.

2

Understanding the Legal Theories of Product Liability

... the juggernaut of modern technology has repeatedly given rise to new concepts in our torts jurisprudence and procedure. Old citadels of jurisprudence have been demolished, modified, and redefined to meet the needs of a rapidly changing industrial society, one which confers on its members both benefits and burdens previously unimaginable. Miques v. Fibreboard Corp.

Longstanding theories of liability for manufacturers and sellers of products have indeed been "demolished, modified, and redefined" during the past two decades. Traditional tort law was based on deterring negligence or culpable conduct and giving reparation to those injured as a result of a "lack of due care."

But a shift has occurred. The trend in the law of product liability has been simply to determine who is best able to pay for an injury and to hand down judicial dictates that will facilitate these societal cost shifts. Fault and standards of care in production and distribution have become secondary considerations.

Product defects are still discussed by the courts, but are reviewed under new theories of liability. A product will still be found defective in one of four ways:

- Its design,
- Its construction,
- Its failure to give a warning (or an adequate warning), or
- Its failure to conform to an express warranty.

An injured party may sue a manufacturer or seller for these four types of defects under basically three different theories: negligence, strict liability, and breach of implied warranty. Under a *negligence* theory, a manufacturer/seller will be liable for an injury that was foreseeable at the time and that resulted from a lack of due care. In contrast, a manufacturer will be liable under a *breach of implied warranty* theory if a harm occurs as a result of a product that is not fit for the purpose it was intended. Under *strict liability,* the focus shifts from the care taken by the manufacturer to the product itself. Strict liability laws vary from state to state.

The entire product liability law is complicated by the fact that in most states, a single claim can be brought both on tort theories (negligence, strict liability, or fraud), and on contract theories such as breach of warranty. What difference can this make? Different statutes of limitation, different remedies, and different levels of proof are required under tort and contract.

STRICT LIABILITY

Negligence and breach of warranty were the only theories under which an injured party could sue prior to the 1940s except in limited cases— such as those involving unusually hazardous products (dynamite)—in which case the courts would impose strict liability.

Strict liability did, however, begin edging its way into the court system about 1910 as a limited theory and was applied to cases involving food. In the 1944 case of *Escola v. Coca Cola,* the California Supreme Court hinted that strict liability might be adopted as a theory to better distribute the costs of product-related injuries.

But it was not until the now-landmark 1963 case of *Greenman v. Yuba Power Products* that the California Supreme Court departed from the traditional negligence standard and set forth what was to became known as the theory of "strict liability." The case basically ousted the concept of fault, and found that a manufacturer could be responsible for product harms no matter *what* care went into the designing and warning of a product.

The court held that a manufacturer is strictly liable where its product "proves to have a defect that causes injury to a human being." This "strict liability" idea was quickly adopted by other jurisdictions, and is now law in various forms in about three-fourths of the states. Thirty-five states adhere to the rule set out in the *Restatement of Torts* (Second) S402A, which holds that one who sells a product "in a defective condition unreasonably dangerous to the user or consumer or to his property" will be strictly liable for harm to the user.

Other states have garden varieties of strict liability that include elements of negligence. The risks of the product are weighed against the utility of the product in determining whether there is a defect or whether the product is unreasonably dangerous in most jurisdictions. In five states, and the District of Columbia, strict liability has not been adopted.

The rationale for product liability as it has evolved includes:

1. People injured by an unreasonably dangerous product should be compensated in today's society of mass production and automation, despite the fact that manufacturers have used due care;
2. The cost of accidents should be spread among society and to all users of the products, and
3. Strict liability will serve as impetus to business to produce safer products.

Since different states have different rationales in passing strict liability laws, there is a wide divergence among the 50 states as to defenses, definitions of design defects, who can recover, potential defendant liability, punitive damages, and the kind of evidence that can be offered as proof against the manufacturer/seller.

WHAT IS A DEFECT?

The majority of courts agree that a manufacturer has a duty to design a product that is free from defects. But the courts differ considerably in defining just what a defect is.

As noted, some courts require proof that the design defect rendered the product unsafe if it is "unreasonably dangerous." Others do not. In Arizona, a court will find a product's design adequate if it conforms to the "technical, mechanical, and scientific knowledge of designing in existence and is reasonably feasible for use at the time" the product leaves the plant.

In California, the test focuses on the consumer. If the product fails "to perform as safely as an ordinary consumer would have expected," the manufacturer will be held liable.

One of the most important considerations in a test for defectiveness is the manufacturer's ability—within practical and technological limits—to improve the safety of the product. The courts generally will weigh evidence of whether a product conforms with industry custom. But that is not an absolute defense. In some instances, the courts will find that the entire industry may have been at fault in not developing and designing a "safer" product.

Another factor considered is whether the product user anticipated the dangers of the product. The longstanding rule had been that a manufacturer did not have to warn or guard against an "open and obvious" dangerous condition of a product. While some courts still adhere to this view, there has been a move away from this concept. Unless the danger of a product is almost universal common knowldge, a product must be designed to prevent against even obvious dangers.

PRODUCT DEFECTS

A product generally is considered to be unsafe in construction if it deviates from the manufacturer's design or performance specifications. Strict liability was adopted in this area because injured parties were not able to show that a manufacturer knew or should have known that the product was unsafe. It was merely an aberration of the industrial society.

As a result, most states will find a manufacturer strictly liable if his product differs from all others off the assembly line or if it differs from design specifications and someone is injured. Most commentators do not criticize application of strict liability standards to manufacturing defects since modern quality control can rid the system of most errors and those that can't be remedied can be insured against. Further, most believe these standards produce inequitable solutions. In choosing between two innocent parties—an innocent user who is injured and a manufacturer who unknowingly produces a so-called lemon (a product differing from others)—the manufacturer should be liable.

In many jurisdictions, wholesalers, retailers, and distributors are held to the same standards of liability as manufacturers. The result is that product sellers are frequently named in a suit, despite the fact that they had nothing to do with the product harm. They are forced to litigate, despite their innocence.

FAILURE TO WARN OF POTENTIAL DANGERS

Even if a product does not have a defect, strict liability may be applied if the product is "unreasonably dangerous" and the manufacturer fails to give proper warnings of the product dangers or proper instructions as to its use.

The less obvious the danger, the more likely the courts will be to require a warning. For instance, it was held that a manufacturer of a polio vaccine was required to warn that there was a risk of contracting polio from the vaccine—even though the risk was less than a million to one.

A duty to warn may be required even where the defendant's use of the product is abnormal. An example: One court held the manufacturer of furniture polish liable for the death of a fourteen-month-old child who drank the polish because no warning was given as to the toxic nature of the product.

The desire to compensate victims of product-related accidents has led some courts to impose on manufacturers a broad duty to warn all foreseeable users of almost all possible hazards inherent in the use or misuse of a product.

In 1982, the Supreme Court of New Jersey went to the extreme in a product liability warning case holding that strict liability would be imposed for failure to warn of product risks irrespective of whether those risks were scientifically discoverable, and therefore knowable, at the time of the failure *(Beshada v. Johns-Manville Products Corp.*, 90 NJ A2D 191, 477, 539 (1982).

LEGAL CONSIDERATIONS

Defenses. In negligence cases, defenses to a product liability action can include assumption of the risk and contributory negligence. In some states, if a plaintiff knowingly assumed the risk or contributed to his/her own injury, recovery will be completely barred. The majority of states have a qualified comparative fault system. Under this system, a claimant can only recover if his or her fault did not exceed that of the defendant. Another 13 states allow pure comparative responsibility to apply and split the costs in proportion to the degree of fault of each party. Thus, if a plantiff was found to have contributed to his own harm by 30 percent and the manufacturer by 70 percent, the plantiff would get only 70 percent of damages awarded.

California, and a few other states which have strict liability, allow comparative fault to be applied to the damage award. Others do not.

Punitive damages. The majority of states permit a jury to award punitive damages. Proof must be made that any injury resulted from the defendant's intentional or reckless disregard for the safety of others. Punitive damages are imposed to punish a flagrantly careless behavior or the intentional acts of a company to put a product on the market it knows is faulty. Few rules are applied as to the amount of money a jury can award.

Statute of limitation/repose. Statutes of limitation set a time limit within which a party can bring a suit once an injury occurs or is discovered. States differ, but generally a suit must be filed within one to three years. Statutes of repose differ in that they set a time limit in which a suit can be brought once a product has been sold. Some states have no such time limit, so that a manufacturer or seller could be held liable for injuries caused by a product they produced or sold 40 years ago. Still other states set short time periods such as 10 or 12 years. The one extreme puts an undue burden on the manufacturer, particularly those which produce industrial goods and tools that last for decades. The other extreme often unduly limits the rights of an injured party.

WARRANTY (CONTRACT) THEORIES: EXPRESS AND IMPLIED

In addition to strict liability and negligence theories, a manufacturer can be held liable under warranty (contract) theories. There are two kinds of warranties—express and implied. An express warranty is a specific representation about the characteristics of the product. Puffery, or mere opinion of the product, is generally not considered an express warranty. For instance, "This is the best toothpaste on the market today," is generally considered "mere opinion" and not a warranty.

Express warranties are created by

1. An affirmative promise or guarantee of fact (this is nonbreakable) relating to the product, which induces the buyer to make a purchase;
2. A description of the product, which is made a part of the bargain, and
3. A sample or model.

Note that the words "guarantee" or "warranty" are not necessary for the court to find that an express warranty was made.

In order for an injured party to have a cause of action under an express warranty theory, the purchaser had to have relied on the promise. A misrepresentation must be proved. The representation must have been made prior to or during the sale of the product, but it could be an oral promise, as well as a written one. In general, a manufacturer or seller will be strictly liable if he expressly warrants that a product will perform a certain way and it does not.

An implied warranty is one which the court imputes to every product. It is neither written nor based on statements to the seller. Under the *Uniform Commercial Code*, which applies to all goods, a product is expected to have a "warranty of merchantability" and a "warranty of fitness."

The warranty of merchantability simply guarantees the product for ordinary use. For goods to be merchantable (Section 2-314 of the UCC):

- They must fit the ordinary purposes for which the goods are used;
- Each unit must be (with variations permitted by contract) of the same kind, quality, and quantity;
- They must be adequately packaged and labeled as the agreement may require;
- They must conform to any express promises;
- And, in the case of fungible goods, they must be of fair or average quality.

An implied warranty of fitness guarantees a product for a specified use. It is attached only when the seller knows (or has reason to know) how the purchaser intends to use the product and when the purchaser relies on the seller's judgment that the product would satisfy that use.

Implied warranties may be disclaimed in writing and upheld if those disclaimers are readily understood. However, it is virtually impossible to disclaim express warranties.

TRENDS IN STRICT LIABILITY

Different states give different people causes of action. While all states give users and consumers of products a cause of action, only 16 states allow an injured bystander to bring an action. A few other states permit a foreseeable bystander to bring an action.

Two states, California and New York, permit evidence of post-accident remedial measures to show the product was defective prior to those remedial measures. All other states adhere to a contrary common-law rule.

Punitive damage provisions differ among the states, with some requiring that the damages be awarded in proportion to the compensatory damages. Four states—Louisiana, Massachusetts, Nebraska, and Alaska—don't allow any punitive damages.

In 15 states, a "state of the art" defense is permitted, allowing a manufacturer to prove that the most up-to-date technology was used at the time the product was produced. The rest do not adhere to this defense. In many of those states where it is not allowed, state-of-the-art evidence is allowed to show whether a product was "unreasonably dangerous."

California recently held that a person can recover for mental distress even where there is no physical injury. Thus, a person who witnesses a car accident may be able to recover against the manufacturer of the car.

New York introduced the "enterprise theory of liability" in a 1980 case, holding that when it is impossible to identify a specific manufacturer of a generically manufactured product, all leading manufacturers can be held jointly and severally liable. A similar theory, called the market share theory, has been adopted in California. Under the market share theory, each manufacturer is liable for the share of the judgment in proportion to his percentage share of the product market.

3

Product Liability Prevention

Every company wants to avoid the financial burdens that accompany product liability litigation. If a company is not large enough or financially secure enough to self-insure against these risks, it will turn to the commercial insurance market. There it will want to find comprehensive coverage at the lowest possible price, which will depend upon the insurer's judgment about the company as a risk. Before negotiating insurance arrangements, a company needs to assess its risk posture.

Once insured, other concerns remain: possible damage to the company's reputation, those litigation-related costs not covered by insurance, the threat of being reclassified as a high insurance risk, and the general disruption that tends to accompany the filing of product liability claims. The objective is to control these potentially skyrocketing costs.

Prevention is the first defense in controlling litigation-related costs. And for guidance, manufacturers and sellers of products must turn to the law. In theory, this requires a relatively straightforward interpretation of legal guidelines.

In practice, however, this is no easy task. There are no clear, precise legal guideposts. In each case, the issue is determined by what the company should have known about its product's safety-worthiness and whether this actual or imputed knowledge led to informed, reasonable, protective decisions under those particular circumstances.

This chapter attempts to merge the retrospective, judicial decision-making process with the company's prospective judgments. Those factors that are certain to go into the court's evaluation are suggested as the best available guideposts for translating the law into action.

PRODUCT QUALITY: MINIMIZING DEFECTS IN CONSTRUCTION

For manufacturing/construction defects, strict liability is the rule—liability without fault. It is almost certainly to remain the rule, even if uniform product liability law is adopted. Translated into a company's preventative legal duties for product safety, this leaves no room for error, irrespective of how reasonable product quality efforts have been. While a fail-safe program for product quality control is unlikely, liability for manufacturing defects can be minimized by measuring a company's preventative actions within the following guidelines:

• Each component of the product should be checked to ensure its reliability and integrity at every stage of production. If possible, have a second-line defense against errors in the inspection or testing process to ensure that an avoidable mistake will not be the source of liability.

• Some documentation should be made at each level of inspection and testing, particularly at the final stage. Checklists are useful tools when they cover each aspect subject to inspection and testing. Some companies even take pictures—remember, it's likely to be the claimant's word against the company's proof.

• Evaluate current production procedures to determine potential causes of construction defects. Inspect machinery, processes, and procedures regularly to ensure proper functioning. If possible, build back-up inspections and tests into the systems.

• Train inspectors and testers properly and make sure that inspection and testing procedures are clear and unambiguous. Train supervisory personnel thoroughly. To the extent possible, maximize oversight of inspections and tests.

- Design layers of quality-control supervisory responsibility up to top management levels. Consider proper disciplinary actions for breakdowns at any level. Some companies use review boards to recommend possible sanctions and include employees in the process. Be aware of any labor-relations complications, however, and, if appropriate, check with counsel before implementing this phase of the program.
- Whenever possible, involve employees in every level of the program and consider incentives for excellence.
- Be aware that any responsibility for final inspections cannot be delegated to distributors, wholesalers, or dealers. Courts have held this duty undelegable.
- Regard packaging as part of the product itself and subject it to the same inspections and tests as the product and its components. Consider the effects that handling and shipping will have on the integrity of the product and its components.
- Design tests and inspections to cover the most adverse foreseeable product uses.

DESIGN REVIEWS: UP-FRONT DESIGN OF SAFETY INTO THE PRODUCT

In design cases, the majority of courts apply some form of fault-based standard, even if they call it strict liability. Risks are generally weighed against product benefits. Thus, a company must ensure that a product's design meets the best available state-of-the-art technology. Economic infeasibility may or may not influence the court. At the very minimum, however, the following factors should be considered.

- During all phases of research and preparation of design specifications, evaluate any reasonably foreseeable hazards of intended use and reasonably expected misuse. The ideal is to maximize safety through product design.
- Evaluate each potential component of the product and the relative impacts of each upon the safety of the final product. Consider the probable impacts and possible consequences of a failure of even the most insignificant part.

• Identify and review all applicable existing or pending federal, state, local, or voluntary standards which may affect the product's design or use. Consider these as minimally acceptable criteria.

• Accumulate and evaluate available information about similar or proposed products and analyze any problem. This should include evaluating court cases involving like products and situations.

• If possible, design a number of alternative specifications and evaluate the relative advantages and disadvantages of each.

• Up front, consider the way the product will be shipped or handled and whether this could affect the safety-worthiness of design features.

• Once a proposed design is completed, have it evaluated and reviewed internally as comprehensively as possible to ensure that nothing has been missed. Some companies use a committee for this purpose.

• Identify applicable governmental regulations and industry practices as a beginning point for testing standards. Consider having the product design or prototype reviewed, tested, or certified by any available outside accredited testing laboratory.

• Build into the manufacturing process—whenever possible—a component coding system. In this way, outside suppliers can be identified, if necessary, at some future time.

LABELING, WARNING, AND INSTRUCTIONS

Some products, no matter how safely designed and manufactured, can be hazardous if not used properly. These products should be accompanied by easily understood warnings. It is particularly important to provide comprehensive warnings, both because of the soaring number of product liability cases based on failure-to-warn theories and as a simple marketing strategy.

Warnings can be issued by means of labels, brochures, packaging materials, or instruction manuals. The law requires manufacturers to warn users of any potential dangers which can result in harm. In general, obvious hazards provide their own notice and do not require special labeling. But just what is obvious has become increasingly hazy in the courtroom as judges move toward strict liability.

For instance, a jury returned a $2 million verdict against a manufacturer who failed to include a warning that operating a crane cab near power lines could be dangerous. The manufacturer argued that it was an obvious danger to a trained driver and a warning was not required. But, in at least one state, that argument did not win. Two other states, in exactly similar cases, ruled that such a warning need not be given.

Once it is decided that a warning is necessary, you must decide what is an adequate warning. Generally, the warning should explain the risk involved, describe the nature of the risk, provide the user with information to avoid the hazard, and communicate to the person exposed to the hazard.

Often the courts will hold that you must warn against unintended uses of a product. In a case involving a 14-year-old boy who died from inhaling the Freon propellant in a spray greaseless frying product, the court held that a label stating, "Avoid direct inhalation of concentrated vapors. Keep out of reach of children," was inadequate.

The court said the warning had to be "comprehensible to the average user and convey a fair indication of the nature and extent of the danger to the mind of a reasonably prudent person."

While there is no exact set of rules about what constitutes an adequate warning, there are some guidelines which will serve as starting points.

Identifying Your User

Warnings must be designed differently if there is a possibility that illiterates, children, non-English speaking persons, or handicapped individuals will use the product. And the more serious the potential for harm, the more important it is that all potential users (or misusers) be informed about dangers. The result is that the courts have often held that words alone are not enough to provide adequate warning. Pictures, too, may be required.

For instance, poison or cleaning products which could fall into the hands of children should be accompanied by a pictorial as well as a verbal warning. Some warnings should be spelled out in two languages.

Practical Considerations in Designing Labels and Warnings

A number of agencies, including the Food and Drug Administration, the Department of Health Education and Welfare, the Federal Trade Commission, the Consumer Product Safety Commission, the Department of Labor, and the Department of Transportation—to name a few—have regulations regarding the preparation of labels. You should be aware of the agency regulations that apply to your product. Failure to comply with regulations can result in government-ordered recalls, fines, higher product liability insurance premiums, and repair costs.

Be aware, however, that complying with all government regulations is not a bar to civil tort liability. Government regulations set minimum standards, *not* the outer limits of safety compliance.

Some general standards which will be helpful:

- Use language that is easily understood.
- Use boldface type to emphasize cautions, dangers, and warnings.
- Use special hazard symbols as needed to reinforce the written word.
- Carefully locate labels or warnings on the product near the potential hazard area so that it will be seen.
- Design the warning to attract attention.
- If you provide a label, make sure it will last for the life of the product.
- Design the warnings so that they identify the hazard, reveal consequences of use or misuse, and provide instructions to avoid the hazard.
- Update warnings as called for. Recalls may be necessary.
- Consider how you can best communicate warnings to second owners.
- Avoid negative words such as "not," "except," or "unless."
- Evaluate your labels to ensure that they accomplish the goals you set. Consider a test that involves customer evaluation of the label.

A manufacturer is not required to warn against every possible avoidable danger. But those dangers which are not remote, unknown, reasonably foreseeable, or obvious must be warned against. And, in some courts, even obvious and open dangers are required. In summary, it is important to review government standards, consider all potential risks, consider all potential users, and warn against as many hazards as is feasible. You cannot, in general, disclaim liability.

Instruction Manuals

Instructions should discuss safe methods of operation and precautions to be taken to avoid injury. They may also contain warnings against altering the design of the product, using unauthorized parts, or having untrained personnel repair the product.

As in labels and other warnings, the instructions should be geared toward the audience which will read them. Language should be simple and straightforward. Warnings of foreseeable misuse, improper maintenance, alterations, and modifications should be included. Illustrations and bold print should be used wherever necessary.

It is important that the warnings and instructions go to the ultimate user of the product. If someone other than the ultimate user receives the instructions, such as an installer, the manufacturer may want to consider obtaining a hold-harmless agreement that would hold the installer responsible for failing to comply with the instructions.

ADVERTISING AND MARKETING

In those states which have strict liability, a manufacturer will be liable if his advertising, labeling, or other communication contains a material misrepresentation of fact about the quality of the product and the user justifiably relies on the material. This rule will apply even if the manufacturer does not make the misrepresentation negligently or fraudulently. And it may apply even if the product contains no defect, but the consumer relies on an untrue statement.

Other states have truth in advertising laws, often detailing what must be included and what is prohibited. At the federal level, the Magnuson-Moss bill and the Federal Trade Commission Act provide guidelines on warranties.

Statements made in advertisements are considered warranties and must be treated as such. Disclaimers in other material will not lessen the impact of the advertisement. The advertisement should be truthful, give an accurate description of the goods, make any caveats necessary by law, and be unambiguous. Again, anyone who creates and approves ads for your company should be aware of the legal ramifications of misstatements or overstatements.

REVIEWING EXISTING PRODUCTS: MINIMIZING THE IMPACT OF MISJUDGMENTS AND ERRORS

Not all errors of judgment or lapses in a prevention program will result in the filing of actionable claims. In some instances, a company may have the opportunity to take action before a product liability claim is filed. The following procedures should be instituted:

• Establish a feedback system containing procedures by which field and service personnel or connected product handlers pass on any and all information they may obtain concerning the possible hazards of the product.

• Maintain a list of these contacts and any correspondence in a central source, and make sure that employees know who the contacts are, should inquiries come to them.

• Investigate this information and any other information available through consumers or industrial users to confirm its validity.

• Keep up to date on any research being conducted on any aspect of the product's safety and reliability and on any possible problems that other companies are experiencing. In addition, keep on top of any changes that are being made to products of the same or a similar nature and know what the state of the art is for all aspects of design and production.

• Establish a workable procedure to swing into action if any information would indicate the need to halt further production of products of an unsafe nature. (Evidence of post-manufacturing changes in the product's design and safety features is not admissible as evidence in most states, but check with counsel on this point.)

• Test these procedures, if possible, to ensure that they can be relied upon if necessary.

- Be ready for possible mandatory or voluntary product recalls and develop an appropriate procedure.
- Respond to any consumer complaint or information which is obtained and place this material in the company's records.

RECALLS: SOMETIMES A COSTLY "MUST"

It is estimated that as many as 25 million products will be recalled each year and will cost business several billion dollars annually. No one is immune from the possibility of recalls.

In 1982, Rolls Royce recalled 6,000 cars to replace brake fluid. A massive, multimillion-dollar recall was ordered of Tylenol, following findings that some bottles of the headache and pain drug had been tampered with. Ford, Chrysler, General Motors, Honda, and Cadillac have all launched major recalls for various problems involving automatic transmissions, seat belts, fuel systems, brakes, and a myriad of other problems.

As early as 1974, more than 25 percent of the companies producing consumer goods and listed on the *Fortune* 500 list had been involved in some recall campaign. Today, recalls are a business reality and a necessity.

According to Roy Chapin, chairman of the board of American Motors Corp., "The subject of product recalls, and the decisions involved, can be complex indeed. Yet the fundamental management issue which underlies product recalls is expressed by the venerable truth of the competitive market—that is, if business treats customers fairly, customers treat business fairly."

And customers, as well as the government, are demanding that product defects be remedied. The cost of failing to remedy them can be staggering if injuries result and suits are brought against a company (not to mention loss of reputation and declining sales).

To be prepared, companies should have recall procedures. First and foremost, a line of communications must be established between suppliers, distributors, retailers, and customers so that accidents and defects can be tracked. Repeated complaints about the same product should be carefully investigated.

Even before any problem arises, a chain of command should be established concerning who should be responsible for ordering a recall. While a single executive may be the one to make the final decision, it is advisable to develop a committee to make findings and recommendations. Such a committee might include an engineer, design specialist, quality control expert, industrial relations representative, customer service-sales representative, management representatives, and a lawyer.

If a problem is discovered, the recall plan itself must be devised and put into action. In some instances, repair or replacement may be acceptable. Other cases may require money-back programs. Notification plans should be well established. Advertisements may have to be combined with mailings, especially if good records of sales have not been kept.

Since recalls are becoming more prevalent, it is a good idea to consider computerizing sales information with the names and addresses of all purchasers. This will help facilitate notification should a recall be mandated.

Obviously, the cost of a recall will be evaluated in any decision. However, failure to recall a product once a defect is discovered could result in large punitive damage awards in any product liability suits that result.

The increasing cost of recalls is yet another reason to implement top-notch quality control standards throughout a company plant. The more premarketing testing, the less likely a costly recall will be necessary. But, should a problem develop, prompt and orderly action should be taken to remedy it before injuries occur.

It is unlikely that prevention techniques will eliminate the potential for product liability litigation. And any legal reform will never diminish certain fundamental societal expectations, translated into enforceable legal standards, which manufacturers and product sellers must adhere to. Whether structured formally or informally, liability prevention techniques are the only way to translate the performance of this legal duty into action.

4

Organizing Liability Prevention

Product liability prevention programs should identify and eliminate sources of preventable claims before, during, and after production. How this task is accomplished will vary widely depending on the company's individual product and industry needs. Risk and cost are always weighed in designing and developing a product. Some of the considerations evaluated by many companies include:

How Much Time and Money Should Be Devoted

• Evaluate the type and seriousness of possible product risks and the potential for legal liability.

• Quantify expenditures made in recent years stemming from product liability (insurance, legal fees, recalls, settlement of consumer complaints, redesign or modifications of procedures, and the like).

• Research the types of markets which the products may reach (states where laws are liberal, workplace situations where the chance for injuries are greater, environments where a large number of persons may be exposed, and so on).

• Check with legal counsel for changes in the law which may affect the number of possible legal claims or any applicable or pending federal, state, local, or voluntary standard which may affect the company's products.

• Consider company size and various locations or subsidiaries. Evaluate the respective performance of each and the possible need for increased or centralized oversight.

Accountability: Who in the Company Should Become Involved

Preventing liability should start with top management. The backing and full support of the company's chief operating officers is considered essential by most product safety experts.

Given this top-level attention, a secondary issue is where to place and how to disperse front-line authority. Ideally, an expert in the field of product safety would have full-time responsibility over the implementation and oversight of the product safety function. This person would have the authority to seek and obtain advice from all other areas in the company. He/she would report directly to the company's CEO so that the interests of product safety would not be overridden by conflicting interests of others in a supervisory capacity. Finally, the product safety manager would have a budget and staff adequate to fulfill the objectives underlying the company's product safety and liability control function. Short of the ideal, a company can choose from a number of alternatives. It can, for example:

• Identify departments and divisions with some impact on product safety and liability prevention. Utilize available expertise (legal, research and development, marketing, public affairs, insurance and risk managers, engineering, finance, top management, and others).

• Choose a coordinator (full or part-time) with central authority for the oversight of all functional areas of the prevention plan. While the coordinator may hold other responsibilities, and could come from any of the areas within the company, try to minimize any conflicts with other areas of responsibility.

• Consider the formation of a committee, either on an ad hoc or permanent basis, which would bring together experts from the various divisions and functional areas. The chairperson should, ideally, be a member of top-level management.

- Through the committee or coordinator, audit all areas of existing programs or possible involvement in new program areas. Structure recommendations, reasonable ojectives, and guidelines for implementation of the program areas.

- Consider a program to announce these goals and objectives with top management's assistance. Direct these communications to all managers and employees.

- Through the committee or coordinator, closely monitor the implementation of the program and encourage feedback from all levels on quality control.

- If the committee or coordinator lacks particular expertise, consider hiring outside experts. It may also be wise to have outside review of the recommendations and findings to ensure accuracy or to determine whether there is any other cost-effective way to accomplish the objectives.

- If in-house legal counsel is not available and participating at every level of this process, seek consultation from a knowledgeable attorney.

- Record-keeping and safety documentation procedures should be included. Before implementation, seek the advice of legal counsel.

Company Policy Statements

There are obvious benefits in having a formal statement which clearly defines the company's commitment to and responsibilities for product safety. While these statements will, again, vary widely, a typical format includes:

- General language on the company's commitment to ensure the safety and reliability of its products;
- Fundamental goals and objectives that the company has instituted;
- Specific or general delineation of functional responsibilities and activities which are intended to accomplish the specified goals.

Some of the advantages identified as resulting from a clear company policy statement include:

1. Protection of and advancement of the company's reputation;
2. Formal notice to all employees and managers of the importance

of quality control and product safety;

3. The elimination of any confusion over various responsibilities; and

4. Certain advantages in litigation. The most commonly mentioned disadvantage seems to be that in some instances a formal policy statement may limit the company's flexibility.

5

Before the Summons Comes: Documents Management

Documents are two-edged swords. On one side, they can serve as defensive weapons. They are the positive evidence a company needs to demonstrate that a product was manufactured according to prescribed quality criteria, shipped in compliance with the manufacturer's specifications, and contained all necessary warnings and instructions for safe use. On the other hand, they can serve as the "smoking gun." That is, they can be used as evidence of negligence or other questionable conduct by a trier of fact.

As a result of this dual function, any manufacturer must set up a reliable system that will retain necessary records in an orderly and systematic fashion.

METHODOLOGICAL GENERATION OF RECORDS

Many documents hurt the company in future litigation. Depending on the company's unique situation (type of hazards, governmental regulations, and the like), some consideration should be given to what documentation the company should avoid. It is wise to make this decision after consultation with legal experts.

Others have found the best answer to be comprehensive generation of records. However, sound, clear procedures for the management and oversight of this function is required.

Documents most likely to be harmful to a company during litigation are scraps of paper, memos, or pieces of information which never reached anyone's attention—those which never came to the attention of management or legal counsel. On the other hand, the one piece of documentary evidence that could assist the company may be untraceable. It is possible to control both of these problems.

Within every department and at all levels of management, set an established procedure whereby all documents must be forwarded to one central custodian (for instance, a custodian for each department or location). This custodian should be responsible for ensuring not only that all records are collected, but also that independent, personal files are not retained. While not always possible, these coordinating procedures are just as enforceable as a complete prohibition on generation of records and can generally work to the company's advantage.

RECORDS RETENTION POLICY

There will not be space to retain all records. Some will be duplicates or immaterial to any decision making. Thus, the custodian should have clear guidelines on what to keep, what to discard, and what to forward to a specified central source.

Again, developing these procedures will depend on a number of variables, each company-specific. In general, each of the areas covered at all levels of the company's prevention program includes that type of information which is going to be needed to assist in providing the company's case. However, note that unfavorable tests, comments, or any documents which seem unfavorable to the company's position should not automatically be thrown out. Instead, where possible, refute each on a separate document and retain both. Nothing seems to injure a company's case more than damaging evidence which surfaces from "nowhere" and is seemingly ignored.

Include a procedure whereby any record can be quickly retrieved and directed to one central location. Again, this entire area is a matter which should be discussed with legal counsel.

There are three basic situations in which documents will not be discoverable material for claimants' attorneys:

1. Under the attorney-client privilege;
2. The attorney's work product doctrine; and
3. Protections afforded trade secrets.

The limitations and applications of each of these areas must be discussed with legal counsel before having any significance to the company.

6

Insurance Shopping: The Options

The multimillion-dollar verdicts, the diversity in the laws, the increasingly complex products being developed, and poor reporting procedures for tracking product liability costs have all contributed to the spiraling insurance costs for manufacturers and product sellers. The Insurance Services Office (ISO), the industry's major statistical and rate-making organization, reported that in 1975 and 1976 product liability insurance rates jumped 100 to 500 percent, depending on a product's class. Rates have continued to rise, although not at such staggering percentage leaps.

Furthermore, insurance companies have become increasingly hesitant to write new accounts for products considered especially hazardous. Why the reluctance? According to findings of the Interagency Task Force on Product Liability released in 1977, it is because the current product liability system is highly unpredictable.

Obtaining reasonably priced insurance is particularly difficult for manufacturers of products that have long lives, such as industrial machinery. Suits can be filed in some states against the manufacturer 20 or 30 *or even 40* years after the product is sold. Other industries which have incurred dramatic increases in insurance prices include makers of industrial chemicals, automotive components, and pharmaceuticals.

Smaller to midsized companies often have the most difficulty obtaining insurance, since large companies can offer big accounts and/or are able to provide self-insurance. Yet, it is still the minority that cannot obtain insurance. In obtaining insurance, it is helpful to have some background on how the underwriting process works for product liability.

THE UNDERWRITING PROCESS

An underwriter evaluates each potential policy holder to determine potential risks. He or she makes a determination of risk based on information gathered from risk survey forms provided by individual insurance agents or brokers. Generally, the policy holder is lumped into a risk class, so that estimates of future claims can be developed and a policy premium set. Wholesalers and distributors are generally rated at a percentage of the classification of the manufacturer based on the goods they handle. It is obviously not an exact science, particularly in light of recent developments in the law.

Most companies' starting point for determining a product liability premium begins with the product liability rate manual developed by the ISO. The manual divides risks into 417 classifications, based on the type of business, rather than product sold. About two-thirds of these classifications, generally those described as relatively low hazard, are assigned a "manual rate" for guidance by the underwriter. These rates are designed to promote equity among the individual policy holders commensurate with the expected losses and risks of the particular classification. For low-hazard goods produced by smaller companies with low or predictable loss experience, a package policy is generally developed on a guaranteed cost basis. The ISO rates are generally used as a guideline for these rates.

The other one-third of classifications are not assigned a recommended rate; they are left to be determined by the individual underwriter. They tend to be high-risk categories, such as industrial chemicals, industrial grinding and abrasive products, pharmaceuticals, and many industrial machinery industries. Rates for larger organizations involved with higher hazard products are developed by using composite industry rates or in accordance with a negotiated retrospective rating plan. Under a retrospective rating plan, adjustments to the policy premium are made to reflect actual losses incurred during the policy term. These plans are generally negotiated with large companies, those that have more than $50 million worth of sales a year. Often, excess coverage is purchased for these companies from many different insurance companies.

State insurance regulators generally require policies to be submitted to them for approval. However, they do not protect the commercial buyer of insurance to the same degree as they do the individual buyer, assuming that the commercial policy holder will be more sophisticated. As a practical matter, most state regulators allow insurers to charge rates based on their own judgment for those product classifications that are given no "manual rate" by the ISO. Furthermore, excess rates or surcharges can be applied to any policy for any reason, with the insured party's consent. As a result, actuarial analysis has only limited impact on policy costs. Much of the premium is based on judgmental factors, such as estimates of loss frequency and severity.

For those reasons, it is important as an insurance shopper to find out what classification your company is given. You may disagree and be able to negotiate a lower premium based on a reclassification.

DETERMINING BASIC PREMIUM RATES

Factors an underwriter considers when determining what rate, or even what classification a company should be placed in include:

- Possible geographical differences in risk potential, even though ISO rates are determined on a nationwide basis. For instance, companies which market products in states such as California, Florida, New Jersey, and New York—all noted for having lenient product liability laws and high verdicts—may find premiums higher.
- Variation in risks based on the ultimate use of the product.
- The existence of products for which no premium has been developed, but upon which claims may arise. In this case, a higher classification may be imposed.
- A sales base which may not be an accurate measure of risk potential.

If a company is noted for taking extraordinary quality control measures, a product may be reclassified so that a lower rate will apply. Therefore, you should volunteer information to your agent if your loss prevention and control measures are above-average. Educate the agent about your target market, product uses, warnings, and track record (if one exists).

An underwriter may determine that before issuing a policy, a loss survey of the prospective policy purchaser should be conducted. An insurance surveyor's objective in conducting a study is to evaluate manufacturing processes, handling, storage, and ultimate use which could contribute to potential problems. The surveyor may find correctable hazards, which are made as recommendations to the insurance purchaser. Generally, an insurance company will make follow-up visits to see if the manufacturer has implemented recommended changes. Sometimes, insurance policies will not be issued until feared hazards are remedied.

Insurance companies and their surveyors will always look favorably at a company which emphasizes quality control to all employees through regimented and orderly processes. This could be an important factor in determining rates. If you have guidelines concerning safety checks, design evaluation, and reevaluation programs, mention this to the insurance company agent, surveyor, or adjuster.

PUTTING YOUR INSURANCE TO BID

Once you have reviewed your risk potential and developed your bid specifications (general liability, special multi-peril liability, or excess liability), seek insurance quotations from no fewer than three "A-Rated," multiple-line insurance companies. If you don't have an insurance adviser, do it yourself. The more details you provide outlining the desirability of your company as an insurance risk, the better you will fare.

You may want to include a narrative history of your firm's loss history, safety-loss prevention programs implemented, its dedication to safe products, and other specific measures taken to distinguish you from others in your industry. Include photographs, product catalogs, and safety manuals, if you have them. Give the companies a reasonable time to evaluate your request and offer to provide further information, if necessary. Since product liability insurance depends so much on a company's individual underwriter, you may get quite different quotes.

Once you select an insurance company, strive to implement safety techniques that will lower your own loss risk. Request the insurance company to review your rates based on these improvements and your own personal risk record.

COMMUNICATING WITH YOUR INSURANCE COMPANY DURING LITIGATION

If your company is sued or notified of an injury relating to your product, discuss it first with your attorney. Barring some extraordinary reason, notify your insurance company immediately. Failure to do so may preclude your receiving insurance protection.

Cooperate fully with the insurance claims staff. Note that routine steps of product liability claim investigation include:

1. Identifying the product by manufacturer, serial number, and/or lot;
2. Tracing the history of the product after purchase;
3. Determining the conditions under which the accident occurred;
4. Obtaining relevant support information, such as statements from witnesses and pictures;
5. Securing the product for analysis and testing as required, and
6. Determining the additional information required to support or refute the claim.

If you have implemented good quality control procedures and have kept good records, you will undoubtedly be better equipped to deal with your insurance company and any litigation claim.

Note: As a result of soaring insurance costs and unavailability of insurance to high-risk companies, Congress passed the Product Liability Risk Retention Act in 1981. The Act eases stumbling blocks to self-insuring against product liability by allowing sellers, manufacturers, distributors, and others not in service-oriented businesses to create "risk retention groups." Secondly, the act permits product sellers to purchase comprehensive general liability coverage on a group basis, without fear of antitrust enforcement.

7

Once the Summons Comes

The summons has arrived. Your company has been named as a de-fendant in a product liability suit.

How do you proceed?

Selection of an attorney should be done immediately. If you have in-house counsel, notify them. Contact your insurance company. If your insurance policy provides for selection of counsel, work closely to ensure that you have an attorney who is knowledgeable and well-respected in product liability defense.

In selecting an attorney, check on his or her litigation experience, reputation in the community, and specialties. Even among product liability defense attorneys, some have subspecialties such as aviation, pharmaceuticals, or automotive cases. Check with other manufac-turers, local bar associations, and insurance carriers for promising leads, and for verification.

If a lawfirm is selected, find out who within the firm will be handling the case, who will litigate it, and who will do the research. Don't settle for an attorney with little experience if you sought the firm for its reputation and knowledge in the particular area.

Providing Counsel with Information

The better organized the company is, the easier it will be for the lawyer, and the less the company will have to spend on attorney fees. Be prepared to give your attorney the following information in an organized manner:

1. A description of the product,
2. A technical analysis of an alleged defect,
3. Results of any investigation,
4. Analysis of prior similar problems,
5. Memos dating to the time design considerations were made, including trade-offs and costs,
6. Copies of product information such as manuals, brochures, warnings, and instruction booklets,
7. Description of marketing plan and copies of advertisements,
8. Notations on subsequent product modifications, recalls, or warnings, and
9. Relationships between all parties in the line of distribution.

If the company has sales records, provide your attorney with copies of those pertaining to the injured party. Describe, in a narrative form, the history of your company, your quality control program (give your attorney a copy of any quality control in-house manuals you have), and the history of the particular product in question.

Educating Your Attorney

In order to properly defend your case, the attorney needs to have a good understanding of the technical aspects of your product. Management should order all personnel to work with the attorney to that end. Company personnel should be prepared to explain technical aspects of a product in laymen's terms, not only to the attorney, but eventually to a jury. Candidness should be stressed. Since it is in-house personnel who have the technical knowledge, have them volunteer information. The attorney may not even know the proper questions to ask. The quicker you educate the attorney, the sooner he or she will be able to evaluate the case and make a recommendation on how it should proceed.

Coordinating With Other Defendants

Several defendants may be named in a suit. When this happens, you might cut costs and lessen paperwork by coordinating litigation discovery material. At the outset, urge your attorney to enter into agreements to share discovery with the other attorneys.

For instance, all defendants may want to jointly depose (question) the plaintiff. All may want to share interrogatories to save on the paperwork shuttle between defendants and plaintiffs.

Naturally, some of the defendants may have conflicting interests. A supplier may be accusing a manufacturer of being liable and vice versa. This should not preclude the sharing of all documents. Litigation is so costly (and rules of evidence often mandate sharing of information anyway) that it pays to coordinate where there is not a conflict of interest. Discuss this with your attorney.

And as discovery unfolds, you may find that another party was at fault and should be brought into the suit.

When To Settle

A number of factors should be considered in settling a suit. For example, avoiding adverse publicity may outweigh the benefits of winning a suit. The emotional aspects of a case (such as with injuries involving the very young or the elderly) should also be weighed. Especially in states which adhere to strict liability, the presence of an injured party is often enough to result in an award against the manufacturer/seller.

And if discovery reveals that the company's product was designed improperly, manufactured improperly, or did not contain proper warnings, it may again be cost-effective to settle out of court if a reasonable figure can be agreed upon. This should be encouraged. Arbitration is often a way to develop a fair conclusion of a case without getting involved in long, costly jury trials. Again, discuss these possibilities with your attorney. And remember that the company, not the attorney, has the final word on litigation matters.

8

Wholesalers'/Distributors' Liability Problems

Wholesalers, distributors, retailers, and lessors are considered an integral part of product marketing processes, and, in most states, are subject to strict liability standards. In states where all defendants are jointly and severally liable for an award, product sellers/distributors are often named in the complaint. This ensures that if one defendant does not pay, the others will. Ironically, product sellers and distributors are often named because of joint and several liability despite the fact that they are ultimately held liable in only about 5 percent of all product liability cases. In the majority of cases, it is the manufacturer who is ultimately held liable.

Yet the wholesalers and distributors must investigate and defend in these suits. The result is increased insurance costs and increased litigation exposure. Both can be diminished, however, if certain loss prevention measures are undertaken.

Minimizing Exposure. First and foremost, make a senior management commitment to quality control by establishing objectives and procedures to help your company avoid losses. As part of the program, you should:

• Evaluate the product line you distribute or sell. Inspect the products during the distribution process. Evaluate advertising, promotion, and sale of the product. If any of these do not meet your criteria, refuse to be involved in marketing the product.

• Review warnings, labels, and instruction manuals issued by suppliers.

• Educate your sales employees about the product and urge them not to make any guarantees about the product which the manufacturer does not guarantee.

• Scrutinize agreements you enter into with manufacturers and consider requesting hold-harmless agreements. Carefully review sales, purchase, and distributorship agreements.

• Your guidelines for returned merchandise should include details on specific product defects. Promptly communicate with the manufacturer any defects in the product. If a particular product is repeatedly returned, consider discontinuing it.

• Periodically review your insurance needs and determine whether your liability is sufficient to protect you under current legal trends.

Selecting Good Products and Handling Them Properly. Since you are responsible for selling a safe product, you should be alert not only to the quantity of products you sell, but also to the quality. Inspection should be made of a product on a sample basis. Storage and handling of the product should be done systematically to ensure its reliability.

You may want to check within the industry regarding a product's reliability, compliance with government regulation, its hazardous properties, and its shelf life. Do not hesitate to discontinue a product that is continually being complained about by customers. In fact, you may want to consider pulling it from the shelves to avoid a costly lawsuit.

Warnings and Labels. The law imposes an obligation on the seller of a product to warn against the use or reasonably anticipated misuse of a product. Note that the courts will apply that standard to a seller or distributor even if the manufacturer never communicated the warnings. In other words, you are responsible for the adequacy of the warnings, as well as for the quality of the product.

The seller or distributor will also be responsible under most laws for the adequacy of a product's labeling. If it overstates the product's capabilities, fails to meet government standards, is not labeled clearly, or fails in any other way, you can be held liable. Again, that puts the onus on the seller to review labels, instruction manuals, and warnings to see if they will adequately alert consumers as to foreseeable harm or reasonable misuse.

Returned Goods Policy. Perhaps the easiest and most important thing a wholesaler or distributor can do is have a good returned goods policy. Detailed reports explaining why a product is returned should be made and passed on to the supplier. Or, the goods should be returned to the supplier with a request that they provide you with a report. Such reports can be valuable in defending against a potential lawsuit. Keep them for product evaluation, selection, and retention purposes.

Sales Activities, Promotion, and Advertising. Marketing undoubtedly includes promotional and advertising activities. But caution is advised. Advertising and promotional materials should be accurate, nonexaggerated claims and should meet any truth-in-advertising statutes at the state or at the federal level.

Phrases such as "fool-proof" and "safest on the market" should be avoided. The reasoning is simple: If any accident occurs, the plaintiff will say he relied on these promises, yet was still injured. It is advisable to have a lawyer and either a risk manager or other high-level personnel review all promotional materials.

Sales staff, too, should be trained to understand the perils of making promises that cannot be lived up to, especially regarding the safety and use of the product. They should understand the product performance, its proper usage and application, its limitations, and any warning the manufacturer has expressed. They should be cautioned about admitting fault for a product's defects. At the same time, they should be encouraged to provide helpful feedback about product complaints to company executives.

The retailer or wholesaler is liable for the representations of its agents and sales force, so training cannot be overemphasized. Furthermore, an ongoing training program, designed to emphasize both cautionary uses of the product as well as its benefits, will serve as a defense in a product liability case.

Hold Harmless Agreement. Under a hold harmless agreement, one link in the distribution chain promises to hold the other links "harmless" for damages resulting from a product. For instance, a manufacturer may agree to hold harmless the wholesaler or distributor. If all were sued by an injured party, the manufacturer would pay for all damages. Usually caveats are included in such contracts, which outline what circumstances the agreement will not hold (for example, if the sales staff makes untruthful claims about the product that are relied on and that result in the injury).

These are merely contractual agreements between the parties and in no way affect the injured party, who may still decide to sue everyone in the distribution chain. However, the court will generally enforce these agreements among the parties if an award is entered. Even so, in certain instances these agreements will not hold. They include:

- If the supplier becomes insolvent and has inadequate insurance,
- If the occurrence is not covered by the agreement,
- If the agreement is deemed invalid for whatever reason (usually fraud or misrepresentation would have to be found), or
- If the agreement can be avoided for other means.

Remember, the hold harmless agreement can benefit anyone in the distribution chain. That includes the manufacturer. All contracts should be scrutinized to ensure that all parties concur on the agreement.

Because strict liability applies to retailers, wholesalers, and distributors, risk prevention—not risk transference—should be the hallmark of any program. Sales training, returned goods merchandise policies, advertising and promotion standards, product selection and scrutiny—combined with legally binding risk shifting—should all reduce the potential for liability.

9

Legislative Solutions for Legal Problems

In 1978, a man was thrown from a fishing boat when it struck a submerged tree stump. He was killed by the motor's propeller as the boat circled, unpiloted. The deceased man's family filed suit against the manufacturer of the boat, alleging a defective design because the motor contained no kill-switch which would have stopped it. The manufacturer defended by asserting that these kill-switch devices were not available in 1973, when the boat was made.

How should the court rule in the case of *Boatland of Houston, Inc. v. Bailey?*

In Texas, the Supreme Court upheld a jury's determination that the manufacturer was free from liability. In doing so, the court found the issue of whether the boat should have contained a kill-switch one of "scientific knowledge, economic feasibility, and the practicality of implementation when the product was manufactured." It also contended that a negative finding of liability required no evidence of "technological impossibility or absolute nonfeasibility" because any safety device may not be "feasible for use because of the time necessary for its implementation."

Contrast this rationale with that used by the New Jersey State Supreme Court in the case of *Beshada v. Johns-Manville Products*

Corp. (1982). The New Jersey court reasoned that:

> Fairness suggests that manufacturers not be excused from liability because their prior inadequate investment in safety rendered the hazards of their products unknowable. Thus, a judgment will have to be made as to whether a defendant's investment in safety research in the years preceding distribution of the product was adequate. . . . In other words, even if [no one] had actually [known], the hazards would be deemed knowable if a [belief] could have been formed by applying research and performing tests that were available at the time.

While *Beshada* dealt with the adequacy of product safety warnings rather than design, the court left no doubt that this holding may, in the future, be applicable in design cases. Why this startling contrast? Is the law simply interested in seeing the manufacturers and sellers of products insure against any and all forms of injury or illness that might result from a product's use?

The tremendous uncertainty in today's product liability law and the desire to have these questions clarified has triggered a movement for product liability reform. Termed a problem in the 1970s, manufacturers and product sellers now believe the situation has reached crisis proportions.

TOWARD A SOLUTION

In 1975, under the direction of the White House, a federal interagency task force was structured to study the legitimacy of product liability concerns of manufacturers and product sellers. While identifying a number of contributing factors, the task force identified three major causes of the product liability problem.

1. The rate-making procedures of liability insurers;
2. The uncertainties in the product liability tort litigation system; and
3. That some manufacturers were producing unreasonably unsafe products.

In 1978, the Department of Commerce empaneled a second Task

Force on Product Liability and Accident Compensation, charged with the development of options for possible corrective actions.

To deal with the problems of insurance rate making, the task force recommended that self-insurance against product liability risks be enhanced and that businesses be encouraged to band together to form purchasing groups, called risk retention groups, which could more effectively bargain collectively for lower commercial liability insurance. The task force recommended federal legislation.

In 1981, the Risk Retention Act was enacted by the 97th Congress. The Act facilitates these goals. This accomplishment led business representatives (during hearings before a U.S. Senate Subcommittee in 1983) to state that this aspect of the problem had essentially been resolved.

Addressing the problem of manufacturers producing unreasonably unsafe products, the task force recommended developing some form of economic incentive that would promote wider scale implementation of industry product safety programs. The task force noted that one of the positive aspects of the escalation in product liability litigation was that more companies were devoting more attention to product safety. However, it noted that smaller companies had limited resources, including time, money, and expertise, which were all necessary for successful prevention programs. Unfortunately, providing economic incentives to enhance product safety has not received as much attention as the other aspects of the product liability problem.

FEDERAL LEGISLATION TO CORRECT LEGAL UNCERTAINTY

When the task force listed the options available to correct the problems in product liability law, it recommended that federal legislation establishing uniform legal guidelines be considered. In 1979, the task force released the Uniform Product Liability Act (UPLA) as a model.

During the following years, several congressional hearings were conducted. Summarizing the findings of the U.S. House of Representatives Subcommittee on Capital, Investment, and Business Opportunity during the 95th Congress, Rep. John LaFolce (D-NY) stated that "because of the severe differences and uncertainty in the law of many jurisdictions within the United States, it was the judgment of the subcommittee that it is necessary to harmonize and make uniform the law relating to product liability."

But concrete action in the U.S. Congress was to be years in coming. In the interim, the case for uniform product liability law was carried to the individual states. In those states, UPLA was offered as a model for voluntary correction of legal uncertainty.

Unfortunately, no state legislature adopted UPLA in its entirety. Those states which did take action corrected only one or a few specific areas of the problem. Even now, no two states have similar statutes and most that are affected by product liability law believe the confusion is worse than ever.

This lack of state action and Congress' earlier finding that a genuine problem exists eventually led to the introduction of federal legislation. But early proposed solutions were not without defect. As Representative LaFolce noted, the subcommittee's findings did not jibe with "proposals which urge (federal) legislation effecting tort reforms which restrict the rights of injured persons to seek redress . . . nor did (they) feel that a sufficient showing has been made to warrant such severe intrusion into the rights of injured persons."

After more than 45 days of hearings, before six congressional committees, and over a period of seven years, proponents of a federal solution believe that the issues have now been properly framed. Federal legislation to reform product liability law is on the threshold of enactment.

S. 44, "THE PRODUCT LIABILITY ACT"

In 1980, Sen. Bob Kasten (R-WI), introduced a proposal aimed at correcting legal uncertainty. In the main, that early version adopted the recommendations made by the Interagency Task Force. Late in the second session of the 97th Congress, the bill was favorably reported by the Senate's Committee on Commerce, Science, and Transportation but never reached the floor for a vote. Again, Congress had adjourned without adopting a uniform product liability bill.

Early in the 98th Congress, the bill was introduced again by Senator Kasten as S. 44. Almost immediately, an all-out lobbying war was in full swing. The business community and those believing in reform were pitted against consumer groups and the American Trial Lawyer's Association (ATLA).

The Arguments: Pro and Con

Opponents of S. 44 argue that:

1. This area of state jurisdiction should be left for the state courts and legislatures to correct because no problem of a magnitude sufficient to demand federal intervention has been demonstrated;

2. Even if federal standards were enacted, uniformity would not be achieved; current inconsistencies in the law would be compounded because of the necessity to interpret the federal standards in the state courts; and

3. The real objective of federal tort reform is to provide an advantage to manufacturers and product sellers in litigation and that the provisions of S. 44 would make it more difficult, if not impossible, for injured claimants to recover.

Advocates of reform argue that the magnitude of current problems and the prospects for voluntary state corrective actions, through experience, speak for themselves. In fact, they point out, trial lawyers have skillfully played both sides of the issue, testifying before the state legislatures that the problems are national and require a federal solution, and then, in contrast, testifying before the U.S. Congress that a federal solution is not needed and that the matter should be left for the states to correct.

Proponents of federal legislation acknowledge that interpretations and applications of product liability law would not be totally uniform and predictable if S. 44 were enacted. However, they argue, it seems painfully clear that a single set of rules will offer much more in the way of predictability than a set of 50 different and ever-changing rules.

On the matter of fairness, advocates of reform contend that gutting the law is not the objective. They point out that many changes have been made in S. 44, and that each change has been directed toward making the bill fairer and more balanced in its approach. In fact, they maintain, the bill's progress through the 98th Congress has been painfully slow because of the time and effort that has gone into compromise efforts. In addition, all parties have been invited to offer solutions which would solve a genuine problem, in as fair and equitable a fashion as possible.

STATUS OF LEGAL REFORM EFFORTS

S. 44 was once again favorably reported by the Senate Commerce Committee on March 27, 1984. This time, by a bipartisan 11-5-1 vote. At this writing, the bill stands ready for floor action in the United States Senate.

In the U.S. House of Representatives, leaders have stated that no action will be taken on product liability reform until the Senate completes passage of S. 44.

If product liability reform cannot be accomplished in the 98th Congress, the effort will continue. A federal solution is forthcoming. It's only a matter of time.

HOW FEDERAL GUIDELINES IN S. 44 WOULD AFFECT MANUFACTURERS AND PRODUCT SELLERS

Legal Uncertainty. Under the supremacy clause of the U.S. Constitution, federal legislation would preempt the tort law of each state in all areas addressed by the bill. Where a rule of law is not established by the Act, state law would be applicable.

Standards for Construction Defects. The bill contains a section which establishes strict liability (liability without regard to fault) for those harms caused by a product with a construction (manufacturing) defect.

Standards for Defects in Design. The bill adopts a negligence or fault-based standard for those harms caused by a product with a design defect. Under the standard, a product is unreasonably dangerous in design or formulation if:

(1) the manufacturer knew, or, through the exercise of reasonable prudence, should have known about the danger which caused the claimant's harm, and (2) a reasonably prudent person would not have made the product or used the design that the manufacturer used.

Inversely, a product is not unreasonably dangerous in design under the Act if:

(1) a means to eliminate the danger was not within practical, technological feasibility and the benefits and usefulness of the product to the public outweighed the likelihood and probable seriousness of the harm; (2) the harm was caused by an unavoidably dangerous aspect of the product; or (3) the harm was caused by an unsafe aspect of a product that was inherent in the product.

In essence, the standard requires the manufacturer to exercise the "care," attention, knowledge, and judgment society would require him to exercise to make the product safe" and "this conduct is measured against the conduct of a reasonably prudent person acting in the same or similar circumstances."

Practical Technological Feasibility. The bill defines the term as the "technical, medical, and scientific knowledge relating to product safety which has been developed at the time the product in question was made, was available for and capable of use in the manufacture of the product, and was economically feasible for use by a manufacturer." The standard focuses on what "reasonably should have been done and therefore differs from an industrial practice standard that focuses on what was actually being done."

Standard for Product Warnings and Instructions. The bill provides that a product is "unreasonably dangerous for failure to provide warnings or instructions about a danger associated with the product or about the proper use of the product if

(1) the manufacturer knew, or, through the exercise of reasonable prudence, should have known of the existence of the danger which caused the claimant's harm; (2) the manufacturer failed to provide warnings that a reasonably prudent person would have provided with the relevant factors that the trier of fact shall consider being, (a) the likelihood that the product would cause harm of the type alleged by the claimant, (b) the seriousness of

that harm; and (3) the warnings or instructions would have prevented harm to a product user in the course of reasonably anticipated conduct.

Under this standard, a manufacturer is not liable for failure to warn about "obvious dangers, consequences of misuse, or alterations or modifications."

Reasonably Anticipated Conduct is defined to mean "the conduct which is expected, ordinary, and familiar to the class of persons likely to use the product." The reasonableness of the manufacturer's conduct is evaluated "at the time the product left the control of the manufacturer."

Standard for Product Warranties. The bill provides that "a manufacturer is strictly liable for a breach of express warranties where the breach of warranty caused the claimant's harm." An express warranty is "any affirmation of fact, promise, or description relating to a product" and may be given "orally, in writing, or through any other action that communicates a material fact about the product's safety, performance, or condition."

Evidentiary Standards. The applicable standard of proof under the Act is a preponderance of the evidence—"a degree of proof which leads the trier of fact to find that a fact is more probably either true or untrue." An exception is under the standard applying to punitive damages.

Legal Cause. A claimant must prove under the provisions of the Act that an unreasonably dangerous aspect of the product was a proximate cause or legal cause of the harm. "Proximate cause is generally understood to mean a cause of a harm for which it is appropriate to hold the defendant legally responsible." What constitutes legal cause is left to applicable state law under the Act.

Standards of Responsibility for Product Sellers. Under the Act, a product seller is defined as "any person engaged in business to sell, distribute, lease, install, prepare, blend, package, label, market, repair, maintain, or otherwise place a product into the stream of commerce." This broad definition includes anyone in the chain of distribution such as a "wholesaler, distributor, or retailer." A product seller is liable under the Act for harms caused by:

(1) its own failure to exercise reasonable care with respect to the product; (2) a product that fails to conform to an express warranty made by the product seller; and (3) an unreasonably dangerous product if the manufacturer is not subject to service of process or if the court determines that the manufacturer would not be liable to pay a judgment entered against him.

In considering whether the product seller failed to exercise reasonable prudence,

the jury may consider, among other factors, the seller's conduct with respect to construction, inspection, or condition of the product and any failure to transmit adequate warnings or instructions. The seller is not liable if there was no reasonable opportunity to inspect the product in a manner that would have, or in the exercise of reasonable prudence, could have revealed the product's danger.

Comparable Standards of Responsibility. The bill provides that the claimant recovers the "amount of damages for which that defendant is responsible." Thus, the Act adopts the concept of "pure comparative responsibility," as discussed in Chapter 2 of this briefing.

Workers' Compensation. Under the Act, "the claimant's total damages are reduced by the amount of workers' compensation benefits that the claimant is entitled to receive." In doing so, the "employer's subrogation lien—the right of an employer to recover from a manufacturer or his workers' compensation carrier the amount of benefits paid to an employee/claimant" is eliminated. Also eliminated is the ability of "the third-party tort feasor (defendant) to bring suit against the employer or co-employee of the claimant for contribution or indemnity" —a claim alleging that the employer or the co-employee bears responsibility for, and should pay for, all, or part of, the product liability judgment. This section is "not intended to change workers' compensation laws" and those laws remain controlled by the individual states.

Time Limitation on Liability. The bill sets forth a 25-year limitation on liability, referred to as a "statute of repose," for harms "caused by capital goods that are alleged unsafe in design or formulation or unsafe due to inadequate warnings or instructions."

A capital good refers to any product or component part of a product, other than a motor vehicle, or vessel, aircraft, or railroad used primarily to transport passengers, which is depreciable under the Internal Revenue Code of 1954, and (1) used in a trade or business, (2) held for production of income, or (3) sold, leased, or donated to a governmental or private entity for the production of goods, for training, for demonstration, or for similar purposes.

The time runs from "the date the capital good was delivered to its first purchaser or leasee who was not engaged in business to sell or lease the product or to use the product as a component part." The section does not apply, however, in situations where

(1) the manufacturer or product seller intentionally misrepresented facts or fraudulently concealed information about the product that was the cause of the harm; (2) if the harm was the cause of the cumulative effect of prolonged exposure to a defective product; or (3) if the harm was caused within the 25-year-period, but did not manifest itself until after that period expired.

Punitive Damages Standard. The Act establishes a uniform standard. In general, the Act states that punitive damages awards "go beyond compensating the claimant for his injuries" and can be said to be a "quasi-criminal" type of sanction. Under this provision, punitive damages may be awarded "if the claimant establishes by clear and convincing evidence that his harm was caused by the defendant's reckless disregard for the safety of product users, consumers, or persons who might be harmed by the product." This evidentiary standard differs from the "preponderance" standard used in other sections in that it requires a greater degree of proof, but falls short of the "beyond a reasonable doubt" standard used in criminal law. In deciding whether the defendant's conduct was in "reckless disregard," the trier of fact shall consider

(1) the defendant's awareness of the likelihood that serious harm would arise from the sale or manufacture of the product; (2) the conduct of the defendant upon discovery of the risk of harm, including steps taken to reduce the risk; and (3) the duration of the defendant's reckless conduct and any concealment of it by the defendant.

In these situations, "after a determination that a defendant is liable for compensatory damages is made and a determination of the amount of such compensatory damages is made, the claimant may move for the assessment of punitive damages" and punitive damages may not be awarded in the absence of compensatory damages. If the trier of fact finds liability for punitive damages, the court shall determine the amount of these damages, and "an amount not greater than the amount of compensatory damages may go to the claimant." The remainder would go to a "person, as defined to be a government agency, nonprofit organization, or trust, for a public purpose as designated by the court." Only one "punitive damages award may be made for the same allegation of reckless disregard for the safety of others."

Subsequent Remedial Measures. The Act establishes the rule that "evidence of a repair or improvement in the safety of a product after the time when the harm occurred is not admissible against the manufacturer when offered to prove that the product in question was defective."

Statute of Limitations. The Act provides a two-year statute of limitation—"the time within which the claimant must file his action or lose this ability." The time begins to run "when the claimant discovers, or in the exercise of reasonable prudence, should have discovered, the harm and its cause." This materially changes the law in many states where the statute of limitations begins to run either at the time of injury or when the claimant "discovers his harm."

ASSESSING THE PROPOSED CHANGES IN S. 44

One United States Senator has called S. 44 the worst piece of legislation to have come before the U.S. Congress in the past 18 years. Consumer groups believe that S. 44 takes a big step backward in the law and is therefore totally unacceptable. Even a few manufacturers and product sellers have opted to oppose S. 44 on the belief that more favorable legislation can be obtained and that S. 44 does not go far enough in solving the product liability problem.

So no one supports S. 44? Wrong. Most who understand the reality of the legislative process on both sides know that any one interest group is seldom able to get all of those items on their legislative "wish list."

They understand that the reality of modern politics precludes any other method of problem solution than a balanced, middle-of-the-road approach in which there rest some gains and some losses for each side.

Manufacturers and product sellers in some states, where that particular law may be favorable to their interests, will surrender some of these advantages. In turn, consumers in some states where the law has broken new ground, and perhaps gone too far, will also surrender these advantages. But, on balance, all parties will come out with a reasonably clear understanding of their rights and obligations under the law.

Many of those who quarrel about the "hows" of S. 44 forget that this was the objective of product liability reform in the first place. And understanding the trends in the law toward strict liability, manufacturers and product sellers are well advised to accept the reality of political balance in payment for what the law might become in the years to come.

POSTSCRIPT

What happens when neither the manufacturer nor the injured party is "at fault"?

This question has been a major stumbling block in efforts to reform product liability law. And to date, it has not been adequately addressed.

A possible solution, mentioned frequently, is some variation of a "no fault" liability system. As theorized, such a system may contain two tiers. The first would deal with situations where some aspect of fault is present. Under this tier, the law would operate under current negligence and some limited strict liability theories. The second tier, designed to handle the no-fault situations, would differ both in terms of formality and in limitations on possible damage awards. Under such a system, damage awards would probably be limited to medical expenses, lost wages, and the like, similar in most key respects to current workers' compensation laws.

How could such a system be designed? As part of Senate Bill 44, The Product Liability Act, an amendment was added by Sen. John Danforth (R-MO) which would structure a judicial review panel to research this concept and report to Congress.

Most manufacturers and product sellers point out that any system of this nature would require several fundamental changes in the tort law's conceptual framework. For instance, under current law, awards to claimants for "pain and suffering" are often large; and while strict liability has taken root in some states, a majority of the states continue to require some aspect of fault to be present. The question is, what are the trade-offs that will premise no-fault.

For now, every manufacturer and seller of products should be aware that this debate is ongoing and will continue, whether or not S. 44 is enacted. Each company should be prepared to speak out on this issue if and when necessary.

Conclusion

Discourage litigation. Persuade your neighbors to compromise whenever you can. Point out to them how the nominal winner is often a real loser in fees, expenses, and waste of time. As a peacemaker, the lawyer has a superior opportunity of being a good man. There will still be business enough.

Abraham Lincoln (1850)

Efforts to cut costs are now sweeping through the nation's business community. Product safety and liability prevention programs should not fall victim to this trend. At the same time, courts continue to pursue their journey into new theories of law on the premise that new legislation will create incentives for even greater investment by business in safety and health.

This combination creates a dilemma. Product manufacturers and sellers look toward legislative solutions at the local or the national level to provide a solution. Yet, the legal revolution continues and by all indications, this trend is spreading.

The facts bear out that both legislative solutions and the legal incentives to produce safe products have some merit. But no legislative solution will ever diminish the duty to produce and market products free from unreasonable dangers. As long as consumers demand safety, manufacturers will have to take steps and make the investments necessary to address this obligation. And as long as legal theories bridge the gap of reasonableness and continue to send mixed signals to the business community, litigation costs will continue to soar with the obvious negative impacts in the marketplace.

Any overall solution for companies will therefore take two actions: To prevent the liabilities a company can avoid, prevention programs must be used and they must work. To prevent the liabilities that a company can't control, elected officials at every level of government should be contacted immediately to solve a problem that constitutes a no-win situation for everyone—except maybe for trial lawyers.